PRACTICAL
BONSAI

PRACTICAL
BONSAI
A BOOK OF LITTLE TREES

KEN NORMAN
Photographs by John Freeman

southwater

Additional Pictures: A-Z Botanical Collection; p10, 11 (David C. Clegg, left and Jiri Loun, right); Ken Norman; p7, 18, 19, 20, 21, 93 (bottom right). The author would like to thank Robin Loder of Leonardslee Gardens for his cooperation, and Alan Peacock for supplying pots for photography.

This edition is published by Southwater

Southwater is an imprint of
Anness Publishing Limited
Hermes House
88–89 Blackfriars Road
London SE1 8HA
tel. 020 7401 2077
fax 020 7633 9499

Distributed in the UK by
The Manning Partnership
251–253 London Road East
Batheaston
Bath BA1 7RL
tel. 01225 852 727
fax 01225 852 852

Distributed in the USA by
Anness Publishing Inc.
27 West 20th Street
Suite 504
New York
NY 10011
tel. 212 807 6739
fax 212 807 6813

Distributed in Australia by
Sandstone Publishing
Unit 1
360 Norton Street
Leichhardt
New South Wales 2040
tel. 02 9560 7888
fax 02 9560 7488

1 3 5 7 9 10 8 6 4 2

Publisher: Joanna Lorenz
Editorial Manager: Joanne Rippin
Designer: Alan Marshall
Photography: John Freeman
Illustrations: Anna Koska

Previously published as *Step-by-step: Create Your Own Bonsai*

CONTENTS

INTRODUCTION

It is not necessary to have expert knowledge to get started in the art and culture of bonsai. If you are already growing plants or trees in containers you may have mastered some of the basic techniques. If you have purchased a bonsai from a garden centre, bonsai nursery or supermarket and have had mixed success in keeping the tree healthy, or even looking like a tree, then some practical advice could enable you to develop skills that will improve your understanding and therefore the quality of your trees.

Buying a so-called ready-made bonsai could be just the beginning of a pastime that may well become an obsession. Bonsai is all about making miniature versions of mature trees, using the same type of materials from which the full-size trees are grown. The tree is just one component of the composition, the other is the pot or container, which must be complementary in size, shape and colour; just as a frame complements a painting.

The idea that bonsai is a cruel form of horticulture is totally unfounded, because the techniques used, such as branch pruning, root pruning, shaping and feeding, are all normal horticultural practices used to control and shape trees and shrubs. These techniques may be slightly modified to suit the art of bonsai, but gardeners and anyone with some artistic flair should be able to achieve satisfactory results fairly quickly.

This book is intended to teach you the basic skills required to grow and train your own bonsai, and to achieve the pleasure of knowing that it has been all your own work.

The History of Bonsai

The origins of bonsai are somewhat shrouded in the mists of time, but the first bonsai are thought to have been grown in China about 1500 years ago, and possibly 1200 years ago these miniature trees began to gain popularity in Japan.

They were almost certainly trees collected from the wild mountainous regions of these two countries, which were planted in ceramic pots and displayed somewhere around the outside of people's homes. These were trees that had been dwarfed naturally by the harsh conditions of their high mountain habitats. The earliest mention of bonsai in Japan appears in records of the Kasuga Shrine in the Kamakura period (1192-1333), and there are picture scrolls showing bonsai from the same period. These scrolls actually depicted daily scenes during the Heian period (794-1191), therefore suggesting that the culture of bonsai existed in Japan as early as 1200 years ago. It was not until the beginning of the 20th century that bonsai were seen outside Japan, when they appeared at an exhibition in London in 1909 and caused a sensation.

In the last 40 years bonsai has grown in popularity throughout the world. Local, national and international bonsai clubs collaborate to advance bonsai knowledge worldwide.

A 95 year old Japanese white pine (Pinus pentaphylla), which has grown to a height of 97 cm (38 in).

What is Bonsai?

Bonsai means a tree or plant, or group of trees or plants, cultivated in a container.

The art is in choosing a tree or a plant that has the potential of becoming a good bonsai, and then growing it, using normal horticultural techniques combined with artistic expression, so that it blends with the container to give an authentic impression of nature in miniature. The beauty of bonsai lies in the balance and harmony between the tree and the pot. Although bonsai can be only 2.5 cm (1 in) tall, it still gives the impression of a mature, full-size tree.

Apex must give the impression of being sculpted by the natural elements.

Upper branch structure must blend with the lower branches.

Space between branches is important aesthetically. It also allows light into the branch structure.

Jin – dead branch.

A strong, surface root structure and trunk buttress will give the tree a mature image.

The lowest branch should normally be the heaviest.

The soil surface must look natural and can be enhanced by the addition of moss, lichen or very small plants.

The pot must harmonize with the tree. This tree has a rugged, primitive appearance and so the pot must exhibit similar characteristics.

The depth of the pot should be approximately the same as the diameter of the trunk.

Buying a Bonsai

So-called "finished bonsai" can be purchased from garden centres, nurseries and supermarkets, but for better quality trees it is best to go to a good bonsai nursery or shop.

Below: An indoor display at a bonsai exhibition.

It is at such places that you should expect to be able to get expert advice on the type of tree that would be most suitable for your situation. Make sure that the tree looks healthy and is free from pests and disease, and that the rest of the trees in the shop or nursery look equally good. Check that the tree is firm in the pot. If it isn't, then it means that

it has only recently been repotted and should be left alone. Check the soil to see that it is a good open mix and not waterlogged. The tree may have wire on the trunk and branches, but as long as it is not cutting into the bark it should be all right. If you buy from a bonsai centre, ask as many questions about the trees as possible.

Bonsai experts are always glad to share their knowledge and their advice and tips are invaluable if you are purchasing your first bonsai. Bonsai can be an expensive hobby because it may take many years to produce a good quality tree, but you need not spend too much to acquire your first tree. If you purchase a very expensive tree before you

gain the knowledge to look after it, you may be throwing your money away. It is best to start with an inexpensive tree so that you can learn as you go along. A bonsai collection can also be started from seeds or cuttings, but this can be a slow process. To achieve quicker results buy suitable material from nurseries or garden centres.

Outdoor or Indoor

Once you have decided either to buy or to grow a tree as a bonsai, you need to be sure that you select the type of tree which suits the environment in which it is going to be kept, in other words, indoors or outdoors.

The area of the world in which you live determines the type of trees that you can keep indoors or outdoors. Whatever your climate, it is generally trees that grow naturally outdoors in your area that are suitable as outdoor bonsai, whereas those that come from different regions would need to be indoors or in a controlled environment. The techniques used for training, styling and general maintenance of both indoor and outdoor bonsai are the same, it is the environmental climate that needs to be different. In temperate areas, indoor trees normally need to be kept in warmer conditions with fairly high humidity, which can often be difficult to achieve in centrally-heated homes. They also need good light conditions, but should not be subjected to direct sunlight through a window, as this could result in burnt foliage. The soil must be kept just moist at all times, and must never be watered to such an extent that the rootball becomes waterlogged. This could lead to rotting of the roots and possibly kill the tree. To increase the humidity around the foliage of a bonsai, you can place the pot on a shallow dish or tray which contains a layer of absorbent granules. These granules are kept constantly wet, so that as the water evaporates it drifts up and around the foliage. This slows down the transpiration of water from the leaves, and keeps the tree healthy. Whether you decide to grow indoor or outdoor trees, you can be sure that your appreciation of the art and culture of bonsai will soon grow into a rewarding pastime.

Left: The bonsai garden in Singapore's Chinese Gardens.
Below: An indoor bonsai display in New York.

Bonsai Size

Bonsai can be very varied in size, ranging from no more than 2.5 cm (1 in) up to about 125 cm (4 ft).

The smallest bonsai are known as *mame*, pronounced "ma-mey", and are normally up to about 6 in (15 cm) high. The next size up is called *shohin*, pronounced "sho-hin", and can be anything from 15 – 30 cm (6 – 12 in) in height. The two smaller sizes are known by these titles but trees from 30 cm (12 in) are just known as bonsai, and are sometimes so large that it takes two or three people to lift them. These larger trees are relatively easy to look after, because they are mainly grown in quite large pots which means that watering may not be so critical as for *mame* or *shohin* bonsai, which can be grown in very small pots.

Top right: A Juniperus squamata, 60 cm (24 in) high.
Bottom left: A Juniperus rigida, 25 cm (10 in) high.
Bottom right: A Cotoneaster horizontalis, 13 cm (5 in) high.

Soil for Bonsai

Bonsai can be grown in any type of soil, but they may survive only for short periods if the mix is not suitable. The correct mix of two or three different ingredients is crucial if your bonsai is going to remain healthy for any length of time.

The function of soil is to be able to retain sufficient water and nutrients to maintain a regular supply of these to the roots of the tree. The soil mixture must not encourage decay by storing too much water around the roots, but must allow free drainage of excess water. To ensure free drainage, the soil must be open and hence contain air spaces which enable the roots to breathe. The soil must also securely anchor the tree in the pot, and should therefore be substantial and dense enough to do this. A good general-purpose soil mix would be: 1 part humus matter; 1 part loam; and 2 parts sharp grit. Make sure you find a suitable grit, as you need one that has sharp angular particles but not sharp slivers which can cause damage to roots when repotting. There are many varieties of grit available as well as many other materials which can be substituted for grit. However, these can be tried or introduced as you become more experienced in growing bonsai. Instead of loam, you can use a commercial potting compost but remember this already contains some nutrients. All soil ingredients should be dry when mixed and passed through a sieve to give particles of between 2 and 5 mm. Soil particles finer than this will tend to clog the air spaces and hinder development of a good root system. There are other soil mixtures available that are imported from Japan which are perhaps more suited to the experienced grower, but they provide excellent growing conditions for trees and many other types of plants. There are three varieties available (shown right), Akadama, Kanuma and Kiryu. Akadama is a general-purpose soil, Kanuma is suitable for ericaceous plants such as azaleas, and Kiryu is ideal for pines and junipers. These soils are a little more expensive than normal ingredients, but to keep costs to a minimum they can be mixed with other components such as humus and grit to make very suitable mixtures. Rather than mixing fertilizers with the soil when potting, it is more satisfactory to add them when necessary during the year. Feeding is dealt with in more detail later in this book.

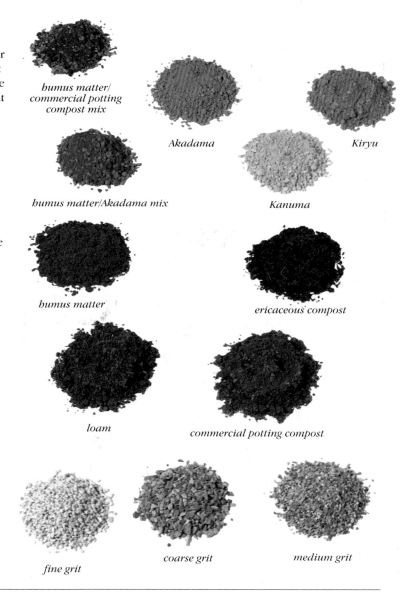

humus matter/
commercial potting
compost mix

Akadama

Kiryu

humus matter/Akadama mix

Kanuma

humus matter

ericaceous compost

loam

commercial potting compost

fine grit

coarse grit

medium grit

Tools and Equipment

A large variety of specialist equipment is available for bonsai, but to get started, just a few basic tools are all that is required.

All you need to begin are large and small scissors, secateurs (pruners), wire cutters, old chopsticks and an old fork . These tools will do most jobs but as you gain experience you will need some specialist Japanese tools. The Japanese tools will make a much better job of all the tasks performed during the training and styling of a bonsai. You will probably buy these tools over a period of time, and the first tools that most people find useful are a sharp pair of pointed scissors and a pair of heavy-duty scissors for pruning the roots. Branch cutters, which make a concave cut that encourages the wound to heal over more quickly, leaving a much cleaner appearance on the tree, might be your next purchase. Once you have a pair of branch cutters, buy a pair of knob cutters which are used to remove a branch or a branch stub close to the trunk, leaving only a small hollow, which encourages rapid healing of the wound. The other tools shown on this page are useful but not essential to begin with, and can be added to your set of special tools over time. Tools should be sharp for making good clean cuts, and free of dirt, so that the possibility of introducing disease into the wound is reduced.

Aluminium wire
This is used when bending trunk and branches.

Branch cutters
These cutters facilitate clean removal of unwanted branches.

Chopsticks
These are useful for working soil in and around the roots when repotting.

Coco brush
This is used for tidying the soil surface, etc.

Fork
An old table fork with its prongs bent will make an effective rake.

Gardener's knife
A strong, short-bladed knife is ideal for cutting into bark when making *jin*.

General-purpose scissors
An ordinary pair of scissors may be used instead of special bonsai scissors.

Heavy-duty scissors
These are proper bonsai scissors, used to trim roots.

Knob cutters
These useful cutters are used for tidying up old wounds and branch stubs.

Leaf scissors
These scissors are mostly used for leaf removal.

Plastic mesh
This is used for covering drainage holes in pots.

Pliers
Pliers are essential when tying trees into pots with wire.

Rake
A rake is used when repotting and to tidy the soil surfaces.

Scoop
This is useful for adding soil to pots during repotting.

Secateurs (pruners)
A pair of garden secateurs (pruners) is useful in bonsai.

Sieve
A sieve is essential when preparing soil for repotting.

Shoot-trimming scissors
These are ideal for pruning back any unwanted growth.

Toothbrush
An old toothbrush is the perfect tool for cleaning bonsai trunk and branches.

Tweezers
Tweezers help with tasks that are very fiddly, such as the removal of old pine needles.

Wire cutters
These cutters quickly cut through wire used in bonsai.

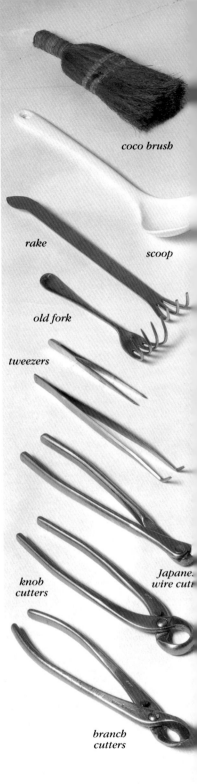

coco brush

rake

scoop

old fork

tweezers

knob cutters

Japane. wire cutt

branch cutters

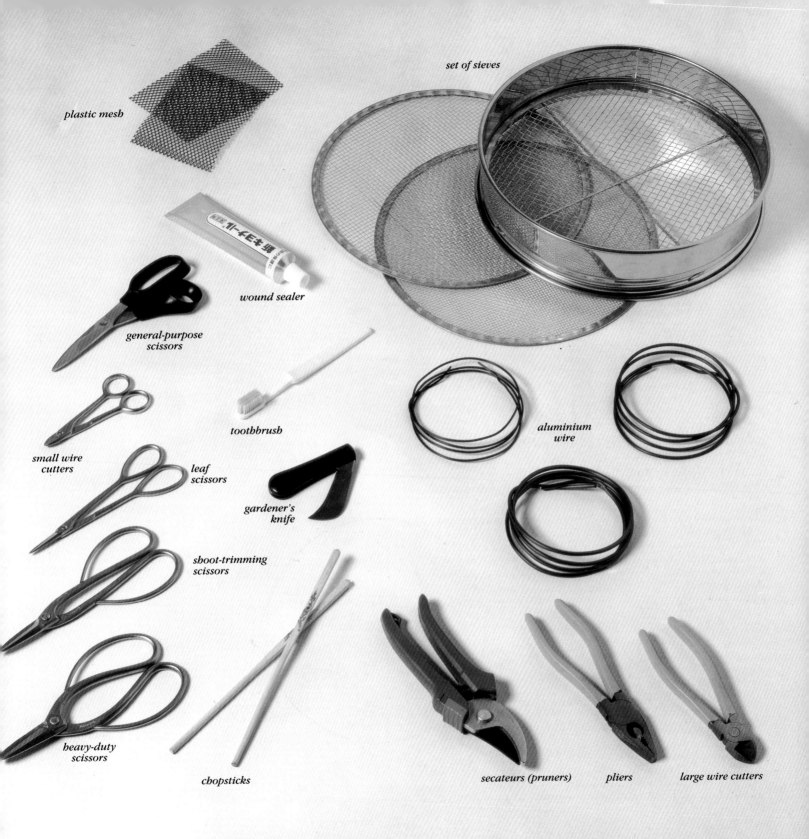

plastic mesh

set of sieves

wound sealer

general-purpose
scissors

small wire
cutters

leaf
scissors

toothbrush

gardener's
knife

shoot-trimming
scissors

aluminium
wire

heavy-duty
scissors

chopsticks

secateurs (pruners)

pliers

large wire cutters

Pots and Containers

The bonsai pot is not just the container in which to grow your bonsai; it is most important that it complements the tree so that the final composition is aesthetically satisfying.

Pots must be frost-proof if they are to be used outdoors, and therefore must be made from stoneware. Pots made of other materials such as plastic and mica will be fine, but are best suited for use by beginners and as training pots. Most people will graduate to stoneware pots eventually, because they give the trees a far superior appearance. You should make sure that the pots you choose have adequate drainage holes, usually quite large, so that excess water can drain away easily. Some pots may have a series of small holes around the perimeter of the base which can be used to tie the tree into the pot. Check also that the base of the pot is flat so that there are no areas where water may become trapped. All pots should have feet so that the base of the pot stands clear of the display stand. This allows for free airflow around the base of the pot, and will promote the health of the tree. Bonsai pots should be unglazed on the inside as this helps to keep the tree stable in the pot, especially when the roots have grown sufficiently to come into contact with the sides. Bonsai pots come in many different shapes, sizes and colours to suit all styles and some examples are shown here.

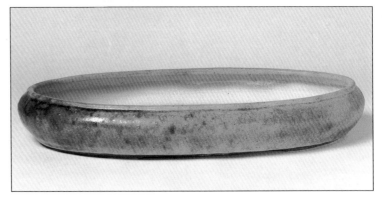

Clockwise from top right: A tall pot such as this one is ideal for cascade bonsai because it allows the form of the cascading tree to be seen at its best. A shallow oval pot is best suited to deciduous varieties, as is the shallow blue rectangular pot. The set of three blue glazed rectangular pots are suitable for both indoor and outdoor types of bonsai and would blend well with maples or figs (ficus) for example.

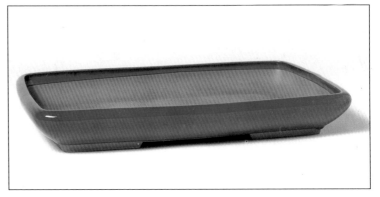

From top left to right: The deep brick-red rectangular pot is suited to a thick trunk juniper or similar tree. The blue oval container is ideal for indoor bonsai such as serissa or ficus. The square matt brown pot is ideal for a cascade juniper and the rectangular matt brown pot is a suitable container for coniferous bonsai such as pines or junipers. A round, dark pot such as this one will enhance a literati bonsai. The round pot, with its decorative rim, complements a flowering tree such as a malus or even a literati pine.

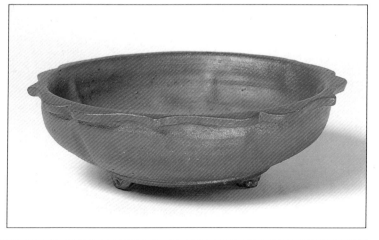

Spring

The four seasons of the year occur in different months in the northern and southern hemispheres. In this and the next three sections the difference in the seasons and the work which needs to be done in those seasons is explained clearly. These are the actions required for tree species that are hardy in temperate areas.

In the northern hemisphere, spring covers the months of March, April and May, whereas in the southern hemisphere spring occurs in September, October and November. In early spring your trees will begin to grow once more following their dormant period in the winter months. This is the busiest part of the year. Most of your deciduous trees should have been repotted in late winter, but if you have any still to be done attend to them as soon as possible. If there is any chance of hard frosts, you should protect freshly potted trees by placing them in a shed or cold greenhouse until conditions improve. Repotting trees should be carried out just before the buds break, so make sure you are ready to repot when the time is right. You can begin to do some pruning now, as this is the best time of the year to tidy up deciduous trees. Without the leaves, it is easy to see which twigs or branches have died back or need removing, so trim your trees now and they will start the season in good shape. If shoots begin to extend, trim them back to one or two pairs of leaves to maintain a compact growth pattern. You will be able to apply wire to conifers, such as pine and juniper, but preferably not deciduous trees; leave these until later in the year. Keep a close watch on the wire on trees at all times of the year – it is surprising how quickly the branches swell. Remove the wire if it looks as if it is cutting into the bark. Do not apply fertilizer to recently potted trees, because it will tend to burn any roots that were pruned during the repotting process. Watering will probably be necessary in moderate amounts as the weather warms up slightly, but be careful not to overwater freshly potted trees.

An Acer – a small leaf variety of Japanese maple – in spring. The tree is approximately 30 years old and has reached a height of 35 cm (14 in).

Summer

June, July and August are the summer months in the northern hemisphere; but in the southern hemisphere summer occurs in December, January and February.

Left: An Acer palmatum in early summer, with its distinctive seasonal foliage. Right: The same tree photographed in late summer, when its leaves have faded to green.

Repotting should have been completed by the beginning of the summer, but if you have a tree that appears to be too large for the pot, just lift it out and plant in a more suitable pot. However, do not disturb the roots: just place it in the pot and fill the gaps with soil. Your trees will be getting well into growth by now and shoots need to be trimmed regularly. Continue to trim deciduous trees back to one or two pairs of leaves and pinch out buds on conifers as they extend. Wire can be applied to any tree at this time of year, but remember to check on wire applied earlier in the season, and remove it if you think the branch may have set in place. You will need to water almost every day as the weather becomes warmer. If it is very hot, you may need to water more than once each day. In any case, check the soil regularly. Feeding will be required for most trees throughout the summer, but the amount of nitrogen applied should be reduced during late summer.

Autumn

Autumn in the northern hemisphere is September, October and November, and in the southern hemisphere March, April and May.

Bottom left: A Fagus crenata in autumn foliage.
Bottom right: A group of Zelkova serrata also in autumn foliage.

The growth rate of trees slows down to almost nothing in early autumn, and the leaves on deciduous trees begin to fall. The inner leaves tend to fall first as these were the earliest to develop. Root growth slows down and the buds that have already formed for next year harden up to prepare for the winter. You can continue to prune pines, but it is best not to prune deciduous trees, because pruning at this time of year may induce a spurt of growth which could be severely damaged by an early frost. As growth has come to a stop, trimming of shoots will not be necessary, except for junipers and *Cryptomeria*, which may require shoots pinched for the last time. You will not generally need to wire in the autumn, but you must keep a close watch on conifers as they have a late burst of growth, and may suffer damage from wire that is left in place. If this looks like happening, remove the wire as soon as possible. It is not advisable to apply wire in late autumn; in fact, it is beneficial to remove it so that the trees can have a bit of a rest during the winter months.

As the weather cools, there will not be the need to water so often. It is a good idea to check the condition of the soil daily and water sparingly if required. Remember that a strong wind can dry the soil just as quickly as strong sun. Apply two doses of nitrogen-free fertilizer, one in early and one in mid-autumn, to harden off the current year's growth. This will help to protect your trees over the winter. As the leaves fall, remove them from the soil surface and display benches so that you do not leave any hiding places for unwanted insects and other pests. Remove any dead leaves that are trapped between the branches and clean the trunks of all algae.

Winter

Winter in the northern hemisphere occurs in December, January and February, and in the southern hemisphere in June, July and August.

Winter may be a quiet time for your trees but it can be fairly busy for you, as quite a bit of maintenance work is needed and, unless you live in a very mild area, you may need to protect your trees from severe weather conditions. Pruning and wiring should not be carried out in early winter, but as all the leaves have fallen from deciduous trees, now is a good time to study the form of your bonsai to assess which branches may need pruning or adjusting next year. Trees that are kept outdoors should not need watering, because they will receive enough water from rain, mist and dew. If they become too wet, however, place them under cover, in the open, until they dry out a little. Your trees will not be harmed by being covered in a blanket of snow: it will actually keep the rootball at an even temperature. Clear any heavy snow from the branches, in case the weight damages them. Prepare for the onset of spring by buying your pots and soil during the winter. You will need these when you begin repotting in early spring. Mix and sift the soil, and make sure you have all the ingredients required. Repotting can be started in late winter but be careful to protect freshly potted trees from any frost.

Left: A group of Zelkova serrata, approximately 30 years old and 69 cm (27 in) high, in winter.

Above: An Acer palmatum, approximately 45 years old and 60 cm (24 in) high, in winter.

Propagation from Seed

Although growing from seed is the slowest way of producing a bonsai, it can be very rewarding. You will know the exact age of your plants and be able to train some as bonsai from the beginning, and grow others on to become larger plants for styling as bonsai. Here are a few tips on starting bonsai from seed.

First, make sure that the seeds you buy produce trees with small leaves or needles and are fresh. Second, if your seeds have a hard case, you will have to chip or crack them to encourage germination, and hardy tree seeds will need to be stratified before they germinate. This involves chilling them to simulate frosty conditions. Mix the seeds with slightly damp sand or peat and place them in the salad compartment of a refrigerator for three or four weeks before sowing. Some seeds may take two or three years to germinate, so you will need to be patient. Your soil should consist of finer particles than normal bonsai mixture and have about 50 per cent sand.

YOU WILL NEED
seed tray
soil
seeds
Perspex cover
pressure board
plant sprayer

Perspex cover

seed tray

seeds   *soil*

pressure board

1 Fill a seed tray almost to the brim with soil and lay the seeds on the surface, spacing them evenly.

2 Cover the seeds with a layer of soil of approximately the same thickness as the seeds.

3 Press the surface down lightly to secure the seeds in place.

4 Spray with water that has had a fungicide added; this helps to prevent the seeds rotting and "damping off" of seedlings when they appear.

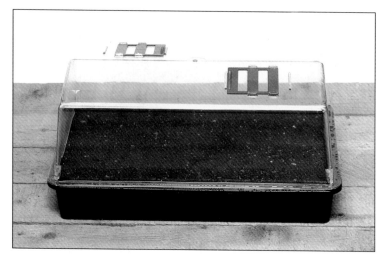

5 The completed tray is covered and placed outdoors, if the seeds are from hardy trees, or indoors in a warm place, if they are tropical or indoor varieties.

Propagation from Cuttings

Propagating from seed may give some variation in leaf shape or colour. If you propagate from cuttings, you will get the same characteristics as the original plant.

Hardwood and softwood cuttings are the two types normally taken when starting bonsai. Softwood cuttings are taken in early summer and hardwood cuttings are taken in the autumn.

YOU WILL NEED
cuttings
scissors
seed tray and Perspex cover
soil
pressure board
chopstick
plant sprayer

Juniperus chinensis

Perspex cover

seed tray   *pressure board*   *soil*   *chopstick*

1 For broad-leaf trees, take a cutting that has several nodes and cut off the lowest leaves and the growing tip.

2 For conifers, take a heel cutting by pulling down on the shoot until it becomes detached.

3 Having filled a tray with very sandy soil, make a small hole with a chopstick for each cutting.

4 Insert the cuttings into the soil for about one-third of their length. Spray with a mix of water and fungicide.

5 Cover the tray to retain humidity and place outdoors in a shady place.

Pruning Deciduous Trees

Pruning of bonsai must always be carried out with care, so that as the wound heals it should leave little or no scar on the trunk or branch.

Basic pruning can be done using an ordinary pair of scissors. When removing a branch, cut as close to the trunk as possible. If you have a pair of concave branch cutters, you will be able to prune even closer to the trunk. If you are left with a small stub after pruning, this can be removed using a different tool called a knob cutter, which leaves a small hollow that also aids the healing process. When pruning Japanese maples, never trim back shoots to the next bud. Always leave 1 cm (½ in) of shoot to allow for die-back. This can be tidied up later.

YOU WILL NEED
scissors
branch cutters
knob cutter (optional)
wound sealer

Acer palmatum

scissors

branch cutters

wound sealer

1 Remove any twigs or branches that are crossing each other with scissors or branch cutters.

2 Now remove any twigs or branches that are growing inwards.

3 Tidy up any unsightly knobbly pieces using branch cutters.

4 Apply a special bonsai sealer to all wounds to prevent fungal infection.

Pruning Conifers

Most of the techniques used when pruning deciduous trees also apply to conifers, but there are one or two extra points that need to be taken into account.

When removing a branch from a conifer, always leave a substantial length of the branch intact. This can be used to enhance the tree by creating a *jin*. A *jin* is where the bark is stripped from the stub, exposing the heartwood which dries out to leave a natural-looking dead branch. This is often seen on full-size conifers in the wild, particularly on pines and junipers. When pruning back conifer branches, you must always leave some foliage on the end of the branch so that there is something to draw the sap. This is not the case with deciduous trees, because they regenerate shoots without leaving foliage in place.

YOU WILL NEED
scissors
branch cutters
wound sealer

Juniperus chinensis

1 Cut out any upward-growing secondary branches with scissors.

2 Using branch cutters, remove any small branches near trunk so that the branch line is more defined.

branch cutters   *wound sealer*   *scissors*

3 Apply sealer so that cambium layer is completely protected.

4 Pinch out the tips of shoots using your fingers.

Annual Pruning

Every year your trees will produce an abundance of shoots from their leaf axils, which if left in place would eventually dominate the appearance of your bonsai.

For trees in training, you may be able to leave some of these shoots in place, if you need to thicken the adjacent trunk or branch, but in mature trees you should remove them as soon as possible. You will need to cut back unwanted growth during the dormant season to allow the tree to develop in the required shape. Prune out branches that are too thick for the design. The tree may look a little bald, but during the following season each bud will produce a new branch and leaves. Trim back any long shoots to a dormant bud and, where possible, to a bud that is pointing in the required direction of growth.

YOU WILL NEED
scissors

Larix leptolepis

scissors

1 Using scissors prune the shoots on lower branches, leaving one or two buds.

2 Repeat the process on the middle branches of the tree.

3 Upper branches are also dealt with in the same way.

4 Finally, trim the shoots on the apex of the tree.

Pruning Shoots

Maintain the shape of your bonsai by pinching or cutting out the growing tips during the spring and summer.

Broad-leaf trees generally produce shoots with pairs of leaves or single leaves on alternating sides of the branch. Conifers vary widely in the appearance of their tip growth, but the pruning technique for each is similar. Spruce and some junipers form small bunches of needles that can be removed using your fingers. Each week, remove the largest shoots, but make sure there is always some fresh growth remaining. On maples and some other broad-leaf trees, you can remove all the leaves in late spring when they are fully developed. This encourages the tree to produce a second, smaller set of leaves, but should only be carried out once in two years, and then only if the tree is healthy.

YOU WILL NEED
scissors

Ulmus parvifolia

Juniperus squamata

scissors

1 Working with the juniper, hold each shoot to be pruned with two fingers and pinch out the tip using two fingers of the other hand. This is the technique for pinching soft shoots.

2 For pruning harder shoots use scissors; angle them so that they follow the angle of the needles.

3 Working with the elm, pinch soft tips in a similar way to that used for pruning soft shoots on conifers.

4 Prune woody shoots using scissors, leaving one or two leaves.

Shaping by Pruning

There are two practical ways of shaping a bonsai. The first method involves pruning in the correct place, in the correct way and at the correct time. You will need a pair of bonsai scissors and branch cutters, but you may be able to make do with ordinary scissors and secateurs (pruners). The second method is by applying wire to the trunk and branches. This project deals with shaping bonsai by pruning.

When pruning, make sure that all wounds are sealed with the special bonsai wound sealer. Select a tree that you think has the potential to make a good bonsai. The signs to look for are a healthy tree with a good trunk shape and a plentiful range of branches. Using branch cutters, prune out unwanted main branches so that you can see the form of the tree. Try to keep those branches that make up an alternating pattern, from side to side, and from front to back, as they appear on the trunk. Finally, prune the smaller branches and twigs using scissors in such a way that the tree takes on a natural form.

YOU WILL NEED
scissors
branch cutters

Larix leptolepis

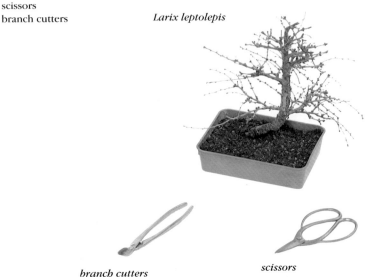

branch cutters

scissors

1 Using scissors, prune the inner branches at the junctions.

2 Cut out any thick branches that are growing upwards.

3 There is a dead top branch in this tree that needs to be removed, using branch cutters.

4 Tidy up unwanted twigs on the lower branches using scissors.

5 Shorten branches where necessary to give a balanced appearance.

6 Trim apex shoots so that the tree follows a roughly triangular shape.

Shaping by Wiring

Wiring is one of the most important techniques of bonsai training, because it enables the trunk, branches and shoots to be positioned precisely. This gives control over the shape of the tree, which, when complete, should represent the appearance of a full-size, mature tree.

YOU WILL NEED
wire
small wire cutters
large wire cutters
scissors

Betula pendula aureum

scissors

wire

large wire cutters

small wire cutters

The technique is straightforward, but requires practice to master. Practise on branches of varying thickness from any tree or shrub before you start on a serious project. Annealed copper is the traditional wire used, but in recent years plain or anodized aluminium has taken preference, because it is easy to use and can be recycled without heat treatment. The gauge of wire needs to be thick enough to hold the branch in place after bending. Check the flexibility of branches before applying any wire, as some species are more brittle than others. Young branches are usually more flexible than older ones. The wire should run neatly on the trunk or branch at an angle of about 45 degrees, and should not be too tight or too loose. Having the correct type of cutters is a great help, as they will enable you to cut the wire close to the tree without damaging the bark. When styling a bonsai, make sure you position every branch and twig. It is this attention to detail in the initial stages that could make the difference between a mediocre and a successful shape.

1 Do a trial run. Take a length of wire about half the thickness of the branch and grip the wire to the branch with one hand, then wind it around and along the branch with the other.

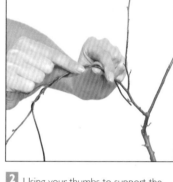

2 Using your thumbs to support the branch, slowly and gently bend it until the required shape is reached. Stop bending if the branch begins to crack. If the wire is the correct thickness, the branch will hold its position.

3 When wiring a trunk, anchor the wire by pushing the end into the soil at the base of the trunk.

4 Wind the wire around and up the trunk. The wire should run at about 45 degrees to the trunk.

5 If there are two branches near each other, one piece of wire can be used to deal with them both. In this way the wire on each branch will help to anchor the other branch in position.

6 Having applied wire to every branch, position them so that a mature appearance is obtained.

Root Preparation and Pruning

The roots of a bonsai are the most important part of the plant. They are responsible for providing the tree with the water and nutrients without which it cannot live, so it is important that you care for the roots properly.

The root structure must always be young, healthy and free from disease, and this is achieved by the regular replacement of soil and pruning of the root system. How often these tasks will have to be carried out depends upon the species and age of the tree. Whatever the age of the tree, the active part of the root system should always be as young as possible, because it is the young roots that take up water and nutrients. Root pruning and

YOU WILL NEED
scissors
rake
chopstick

repotting should be carried out in late winter or early spring, just before, or just as, the roots begin to grow. After repotting, the soil should be kept moist so that the tree is able to support new roots without the fear of waterlogging. You can prune roots at any time during the dormant season, but the longer the cuts remain before new growth begins, the more chance there is of the roots rotting, which could lead to the death of the tree. Pruning the roots will encourage many more young feeder roots to develop, which will lead to healthy growth in the upper part of the tree.

1 Carefully remove the tree from the pot. This tree has a plentiful root system that needs pruning to encourage new root growth.

Juniperus rigida

scissors   *rake*   *chopstick*

2 A chopstick is ideal for untangling the thicker roots.

3 Using a rake, comb the roots to remove the soil from the outside of the rootball and remove about one third of the soil around the roots.

4 Trim the roots from the sides of the root system using sharp scissors.

5 Cut away excess roots from the underside, so that the rootpad is flat.

6 The final appearance should be neat and have sufficient fibrous roots to support the tree when repotted.

Preparing Pots & Potting

Pots should always be clean and dry. If you are reusing pots, make sure that they have been cleaned with a stiff brush and clean water, and rinsed and dried before use.

The drainage holes in the bottom of the pot should be covered with plastic mesh to stop the soil falling through. This also prevents certain types of unwanted pests from entering the soil through the holes. A layer of small stones or coarse grit should be spread over the bottom of the pot to allow free drainage of excess water. When placing the tree in the pot, it is a good idea to make a mound of soil under the rootball, so that when you settle the tree down you know that the roots will be in good contact with the soil. Remember to twist the tree round clockwise and anticlockwise when you are potting, because this also helps to ensure a good contact between roots and soil. When adding the final amount of soil, work it in carefully around all the roots with a chopstick to make sure that the soil is in contact around all of the roots.

YOU WILL NEED
wire
mesh
pot
scoop
coarse grit or Akadama
soil
chopstick

1 Twist a short length of wire into a "butterfly" shape.

2 Place a piece of mesh over each drainage hole. Push the free ends of the "butterfly" through the mesh and drainage hole, bending them back beneath the pot to secure the mesh.

3 Large pots may have small holes in the base, which can be used to secure the tree into the pot with wire. If the pot does not have these, pass the wire through the drainage holes.

pot

chopstick   *mesh*   *wire*

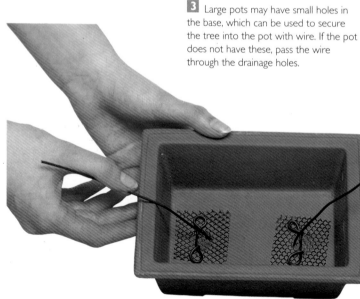

4 Using a scoop, cover the bottom of the pot with coarse grit or coarse Akadama to provide a drainage layer.

5 Add a small amount of soil and settle the tree on to the soil firmly.

6 Bring the two ends of the tie-in wires together and twist to secure the tree into the pot. Top up with soil and tidy the surface of the soil.

Collecting Mature Trees from your Garden

When looking for material from which to design and style a bonsai, quite often the best subjects can be found in your own garden. For instance you may have a small tree or shrub that is no longer required in the garden. So, before you dig it up and throw it away, check to see if it has the potential to become a bonsai.

Bonsai created from this type of material usually make some of the best trees, because they frequently have mature trunks when they are collected. Other sources of mature plants that may be suitable are old hedges. If you, or one of your neighbours, decides to remove part of or even a complete hedge, you may well be looking at a whole row of potential bonsai stock. Look at the hedging plants closely. If they have a compact habit and have been clipped regularly for many years, you could have ideal plants from which to start training some bonsai. Suitable species include beech (*Fagus*), privet (*Ligustrum*), field maple (*Acer campestre*), hedging honeysuckle (*Lonicera nitida*), junipers (especially dwarf or spreading varieties), dwarf rhododendrons and azaleas. Removal of these trees from the ground may take one or more seasons. If they are mature plants, they may have roots that extend for a considerable distance. These roots will need to be cut through with a spade in spring. Insert the spade 30 – 45 cm (12 – 18 in) from the trunk base and make a circular cut around the tree. Allow one or two seasons for the tree to develop a compact root structure, and then dig out with a spade in spring, just before the plant begins its growth for the new season. It may be beneficial to carry out some initial styling while the tree is still in the ground. This can help in the development of the basic structure of the tree. If the roots are cut back with a spade several years running, and at the same time some training of the top growth is carried out, the overall effect should be a better tree when finally removed from the ground and potted. The collected tree should be planted in a training container, using a very gritty compost to encourage a good fibrous root growth. You can use any type of container for this initial growing on process. For example, you could make your own containers out of old timber pallets, plastic storage boxes or discarded washing-up bowls.

1 This is an example of suitable plant material in the ground.

2 The tree can be prepared in advance by digging around the roots with a spade in the season before lifting.

3 Remove from the ground using a spade, cutting roots as necessary with the spade or secateurs (pruners), but leaving a good fibrous root system. Having lifted the tree, prepare the roots by knocking away excess soil with the spade or a rake, and pruning any large roots so that it will fit into its training box.

4 This is the prepared training box. It has a layer of coarse grit covered by a layer of very gritty soil. You will also need to pass some wires through the holes in the bottom of the box leaving sufficient length for "tying in".

BONSAI TIP
Whatever container you use, it must have good holes in the base to allow free drainage of water.

5 Place the tree in the box, work the roots into the base soil and tie in by twisting the ends of the wire together until the tree is firmly held. Having filled up the box with more soil and watered thoroughly, the tree can now begin to develop a new compact root system.

BONSAI STYLES

Formal Upright

The formal upright style of bonsai has a straight vertical trunk with the branches in fairly horizontal positions.

When styling any plant into a bonsai, the first feature to look for is a good surface root system. This will give the base of the trunk a more mature look. Rake the soil away from the trunk to expose roots that will enhance the appearance of the junction between the trunk and the soil. Assess which branches are best suited for the design. Choose a thick branch as the lowest branch and then cut out any insignificant shoots, leaving a sufficient number to complete the design. If the trunk is not

completely straight, apply a piece of wire of suitable thickness and manipulate the trunk until it is straight when viewed from the front. Viewed from the side, the trunk should be angled slightly to the rear as it rises from the soil, and slightly to the front in the upper part of the tree. Decide which is to be the first or lowest branch. It should usually be the thickest branch on the finished tree. Apply wire to the branch, and after running the wire around the trunk one or more turns, wind it along the next branch up the trunk. Continue to wire the rest of the branches and arrange them so that they all complement each other. Trim back the tips of the branches to achieve a balanced tree.

YOU WILL NEED
rake
scissors
pot
mesh
wire
wire cutters
soil
scoop
branch cutters

1 Position the tree in the pot so that the trunk is vertical.

2 Apply wire to the first, or lowest, branch you have chosen to retain.

3 Terminate the wire by bending it back on itself so that it secures the end of the branch.

4 Cut off excess wire using wire cutters then continue with the next branch up the trunk.

Juniperus chinensis — *soil* — *pot* — *scissors* — *mesh* — *wire* — *rake* — *scoop* — *branch cutters* — *wire cutters*

5 Having wired all the branches, gently bend them all into horizontal positions.

6 Using scissors, trim all the shoot tips, so that the tree takes on a roughly triangular appearance when viewed from both the front and side.

Informal Upright

In this style the trunk is not absolutely straight. It is one of the most common styles used in bonsai, probably because full-size mature trees often develop this shape.

The root base must be established before any other work is carried out. Inspect the roots by raking the soil away to expose them. Study the shape of the tree from all angles. When the best angle has been established, support the tree in this position. All bonsai have one angle from which they are best viewed, referred to as the front.

YOU WILL NEED
rake
scissors
pot
mesh
wire
wire cutters
soil
scoop
branch cutters

Cedrus deodara

wire cutters *branch cutters* *pot* *rake* *scoop* *scissors* *wire* *soil*

1 Check for the best trunk angle and prop up the pot with a brick while working on the tree.

2 Wire the trunk and bend until a gentle curve is obtained.

3 Wire the branches and position them to give the tree a mature look.

4 Trim the long ends of the shoots with scissors. Note that the apex follows the same angle as that of the first, lower, part of the trunk.

Slanting

The slanting style is based on a tree in the wild that has been affected by stormy weather and has been blown over at an angle. In the wild such a tree would redirect its branch growth to suit the new growing angle.

Establish the shape and health of the root system and decide which side is the front of the tree and whether the trunk would be better positioned at a different angle. The angle of the trunk should look as natural as possible and the position of the branches must relate to the trunk, so that a mature shape is obtained. When a branch has to be placed in a drooping position, make sure that the junction of the branch with the trunk bends down immediately it leaves the trunk.

YOU WILL NEED
rake
scissors
pot
mesh
wire
wire cutters
soil
scoop
branch cutters

Pinus thunbergii

1 Position at a slanting angle and remove the branch at the front.

2 Cut out the leading shoot with branch cutters.

branch cutters *soil* *pot*

wire cutters

rake

scoop *scissors* *wire* *mesh*

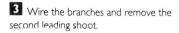

3 Wire the branches and remove the second leading shoot.

4 Finish off the apex by bending it into a zigzag shape that complements the rest of the tree.

Semi-cascade

The semi-cascade is a style that reflects the effect of difficult growing conditions on a tree. The styling here is designed to give the appearance of a tree growing out of the side of a rock face or quarry. Although the trunk line is initially upright, it very quickly bends over into a roughly horizontal position.

YOU WILL NEED
rake
scissors
pot
mesh
wire
wire cutters
soil
scoop
branch cutters

Cotoneaster

First, establish the shape and health of the root structure, which side should be the front and whether the angle of the trunk should be altered.

1 Position at the required angle by using extra soil in the bottom of the pot.

2 Trim the long shoots that hang down below the line of the trunk using branch cutters.

3 Remove the shoot that has grown back on itself with scissors.

4 Wire both the leading shoot and lower rear branch and bend them into place to create the basic shape.

5 Using scissors, remove any backward-growing branches.

6 Finally, use scissors to cut out the leading shoot.

Cascade

As with the semi-cascade style, the trunk line begins by growing vertically upward before cascading over the side of the pot. It represents a tree growing in a difficult situation, such as the side of a rock face.

Establish the shape and health of the roots, which side should be the front and whether the angle of the trunk should be altered.

YOU WILL NEED
rake
scissors
pot
mesh
wire
wire cutters
soil
scoop
branch cutters

Juniperus procumbens

soil

pot

rake

scoop

branch cutters

wire cutters

scissors

mesh

wire

1 Remove this branch because it is growing in the opposite direction to the main cascade.

2 The lower trunk is clean and so the cascading branch is seen to advantage.

3 Wire the trunk and trim out minor twigs, leaving only the main branches.

4 Complete wiring to the end of the trunk, then bend the trunk and trim off any remaining minor shoots.

5 Wire the side branches and position so that a space, large enough to insert a hand, is left between them.

6 Prune the tail to length and trim excess shoots to give a mature look.

BONSAI TIP
A cascade should be grown in a deep pot, and displayed on a tall stand to complement its shape.

Root over Rock

Planting trees with the root system either over or on top of a rock can create a natural and satisfying appearance.

The root-over-rock style takes many years to prepare and involves training the tree's roots to grow over a rock, which is standing on soil. The exposed roots cascade over the sides of the rock and down into the soil, where they seek out water and nutrients. Select a tree that has a suitably long root system and decide which side should be the front of the tree. Choose a piece of rock that has interesting features. Tie the roots to the rock with string, raffia or wire (this will last longer) and plant the tree, covering the whole rootball, including the rock, with soil. During the next few years, the roots will grow closely to the rock, so that when the rock is eventually exposed the roots will be following the rock's contours.

YOU WILL NEED
rake
rock
wire
wire cutters
scissors
branch cutters
pot
mesh
soil
scoop

Acer buergerianum

scissors

branch cutters

wire

mesh

pot

soil

rock

rake

scoop

wire cutters

1 Remove the tree from the pot and rake the soil away from the roots.

2 Expose the main roots (this tree has mature roots already).

3 Find a suitable piece of rock and carefully position it between the main roots before securing it with wire.

4 Trim the fibrous roots into a neat pad and settle the tree in a suitable pot.

Root on Rock

With the root-on-rock style, the roots are grown in a humus mixture and are clinging to the side, or growing in, a pocket in the rock.

You will, of course, need to feed more often than normal to maintain the health of the tree, as the nutrients are easily washed away by heavy rain and regular watering. Because it is going to be placed in a cavity or hollow in a rock, choose a tree that has a good compact rootball. An ideal type of rock to use is tufa, as it is soft and can be easily carved with a chisel, screwdriver or spatula. The tree is then planted into the hollow and firmed in with extra soil.

YOU WILL NEED
rock
chisel
rake
scissors
soil
scoop
branch cutters
wire
wire cutters

1 The rock used here is a piece of tufa, which is soft enough to dig into using a chisel to create the planting hole.

Chamae-cyparis

rock

soil

wire

rake

scoop

wire cutters

scissors

branch cutters

2 Rake the soil from the roots and trim them so that they will fit into the hole in the tufa.

3 Place the tree in the hole using the rake handle or a spatula and fill any remaining space with soil.

4 Trim the shoots on the tree to give the desired effect of blending the tree with the rock.

Raft

This style is based upon the natural occurrence of a tree blown over in a storm. The branches that hit the ground as the tree falls break off, leaving one side of the trunk in contact with the soil. Usually some of the original roots remain viable, and it is these which enable the tree to survive. After some time, new roots emerge from the under side of the trunk, and the branches that remain begin to grow vertically. After many years, a small group of trees will have grown, but they will have just the one root system.

If you can find a tree that has a one-sided branch structure you will be halfway there. If not, purchase a tree that has a good set of branches and cut off the branches on one side of the trunk. Make sure that the pot is clean and cover the drainage holes with mesh. Lay the tree down on the side that has had the branches removed and check the rootball. Using sharp scissors, remove the roots that are on the upper side of the trunk. The removal of half the root system will not harm the tree because you have already halved the number of branches, and it ensures balanced growth. Select the best upward-growing branches to be the new set of trunks, and remove any that do not suit your design. Cover any cuts with bonsai sealer. Finally, select the most suitable secondary branches, remove the rest, position with wire and trim the branch tips where necessary.

YOU WILL NEED
branch cutters
pot
mesh
wire
wire cutters
rake
scissors
soil
scoop
chopstick
wound sealer

1 Lay the tree on its side and cut away half its roots.

2 Apply wire to the main raft.

3 Bend up the tip.

4 Wire the other branches and position them so that they become the new trunks.

5 Using a knife, cut out pieces of bark on the underside of the former trunk; new roots will grow from these cuts.

scissors

wound sealer

soil

wire cutters

rake

scoop

branch cutters

mesh

wire

chopstick

Juniperus squamata

pot

6 Having prepared the pot with some soil in the bottom, position the tree in the pot so that the horizontal connecting trunk lies just above the pot rim and fill up with soil.

BONSAI TIP
You will need to select a pot that is long and narrow or oval for this bonsai style.

Windswept

Windswept is a style of bonsai that would be familiar to those who visit coastal or mountain areas, because it is based upon the form of full-size trees which have been constantly exposed to winds from one direction. These trees have branches only on the side of the trunk sheltered from the wind.

A suitable plant would be any type of conifer with a relatively straight trunk. Rake the soil away from the surface roots of your plant and check their appearance, so that you can establish the best viewing angle. As you are checking the root structure, lean the tree over to one side so that the best part of the trunk and roots are visible from the front, while at the same time taking the branch structure into account. Remove all or most of the branches on the windward side of the trunk. Decide which branches will give the most mature appearance, and remove the others. Position the remaining branches with wire so that a mature windswept appearance is achieved. The tree is then settled into the prepared pot, tied in, topped up with soil and watered. Pots for this style of bonsai are generally round and shallow, with a rough, primitive finish which is appropriate to the natural environment of wild trees.

YOU WILL NEED
rake
branch cutters
scissors
wire
wire cutters
pot
mesh
soil
scoop

Juniperus davurica

soil

wire

pot

mesh

scoop

rake

wire cutters

branch cutters

scissors

1 Using branch cutters, remove all branches that are growing in the opposite direction to the main trunk line to create a mature windswept appearance.

2 Position at the most appropriate angle and use scissors to remove all small twigs and branches.

3 Remove any upward-growing branches using branch cutters.

4 Trim off downward-growing branches to preserve the horizontal line of the style.

5 Wire the remaining branches.

6 Carefully bend branches so that they all flow in the same direction, as if they have been blown by constant winds from one direction.

Literati

This style is unusual in that it has a very tall, fairly thin trunk with just a few branches in the upper part of the tree. One can see the inspiration of this style in the wild where old pines have discarded their lower branches. Indeed, conifers are the trees most commonly seen growing in these shapes, and they therefore make the best literati bonsai.

YOU WILL NEED
rake
branch cutters
wire
wire cutters
scissors
pot
mesh
soil
scoop

The trunk is all-important. It is rarely straight and must have lots of "character". When selecting a tree, you may be able to buy something that has been damaged and is not really suitable for anything else. Rake the soil from the roots to establish their health and the best viewing angle. It is important to reflect the apparent age of the tree, so you may have to make the branches droop severely to achieve this. A suitable pot would be circular and should not be too large, otherwise it will tend to overpower the tree. You may find that a very primitive, rugged pot would suit this style best.

Juniperus squamata

wire

mesh

soil

rake

scoop

wire cutters

scissors

branch cutters

pot

1 Position the tree for the best trunk front; the line should be interesting and not totally straight.

2 Using branch cutters, remove some of the lower branches; characteristically, this style has most of its branches in the upper part of the tree.

3 Remove the heavier upper branches and most other small ones, leaving only about five main branches.

4 Wire the remaining branches.

5 Position the branches to give a heavy, drooping appearance.

6 Use scissors to trim the branches so that a tidy, mature shape is achieved.

BONSAI TIP

Use a round, shallow pot for this style and position the tree in the centre of the pot.

Driftwood

The driftwood bonsai style is not easy to achieve. It reflects the natural look of very old junipers and pines, which have developed areas of trunk that are totally free of bark. In the wild, this may have been caused by natural die-back or lightning. Whatever the cause the result can be very dramatic and exciting.

Driftwood techniques can be used in several other styles of bonsai including literati, informal upright, cascade and windswept. A suitable tree for the style needs to have a fairly thick trunk; one that will give enough material from which you can form the driftwood. Use a rake to clear the soil from the surface roots to check the health of the root system and to establish which side should be the front. Suitable pots for this style will vary, but as the form is rugged and primitive in appearance, the pot should reflect these qualities.

YOU WILL NEED
rake
branch cutters
pliers
knife
wire
wire cutters
scissors
pot
mesh
soil
scoop

Cryptomeria japonica

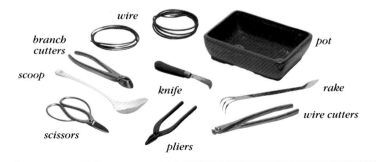

wire

branch cutters

scoop

knife

scissors

pliers

pot

rake

wire cutters

1 Cut halfway through the front trunk with a pair of branch cutters.

2 Break at the cut and pull down to give the appearance of natural damage.

3 Pull off other branches, also leaving a natural-looking tear.

4 Repeat this cutting and tearing technique on the top of the main trunk.

BONSAI TIP

Do not carry out major work on the top part of the tree and the roots at the same time. This could cause too much stress for the tree.

5 Use a knife to help remove the bark, leaving the heartwood exposed.

6 Wire the remaining branches. There may not be many, but those that are left will eventually produce a striking effect.

Twisted Trunk

This style clearly has a strong Chinese connection, as many Chinese bonsai follow it. Ancient Chinese artefacts often bear paintings of trees like this.

The twisted trunk is not a very popular style for bonsai because it does not represent a particularly natural appearance. The trunk is more of a spiral form than anything else and can be achieved by the use of thick wire to manipulate it into place. You will need a tree that has a fairly thick trunk which is flexible enough to be curved into the required form. Use a rake to scrape away the surface soil to check the health of the root system and to establish which is the best side to be the front. Select which branches will make a natural-looking tree.

YOU WILL NEED
rake
branch cutters
scissors
wire
wire cutters
pot
mesh
soil
scoop

Pinus mugo

1 Tilt the tree by resting the rear of the rootball on the back edge of the seed tray. This will give a better appearance to the line of the trunk.

2 Use branch cutters to remove the branch that is covering the front of the tree and obscuring the trunk.

3 Cut out all minor inner branches with a pair of scissors.

4 Using branch cutters, prune out any long uninteresting branches.

5 Wire the remaining branches and carefully bend into place.

6 Bend the rest of the branches into place, and trim away excessively long shoots to refine the outline.

wire

soil

pot

mesh

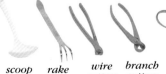

scoop *rake* *wire cutters* *branch cutters* *scissors*

Exposed Root

The roots of many trees are uncovered by years of exposure to the natural elements such as rain and wind. Some elderly trees have a large number of roots exposed, so that the tree looks as if it is standing on stilts.

In the exposed-root style, you are trying to copy a natural appearance, just as you are with all bonsai, whatever the style. Indeed, the first task you must carry out to turn a garden-centre plant into a bonsai is to rake the surface soil away from the roots to expose some of them. This gives the lower part of the tree a mature and established look. You must find a tree that has long mature roots in the pot which you can discover by probing into the soil before you buy. Virtually any species of tree may be used and a suitable pot would be simple and rugged.

YOU WILL NEED
rake
brush
scissors
pot
mesh
wire
soil
scoop
chopstick
branch cutters

1 Remove the tree from the pot.

2 Rake the soil away from the roots.

3 Brush the main roots clean.

4 Trim the fibrous rootball so that the bottom is neat and flat.

5 Settle the tree into a prepared pot with the best roots to the front.

Acer buergerianum

soil

pot

scoop

mesh

chopstick

rake

scissors

branch cutters

wire

6 Fill up with soil and work in and around the roots with a chopstick.

BONSAI TIP
As with all bonsai, the final appearance of a tree can be improved by adding some moss to the surface of the soil.

Clump

There are several ways that this design can be created, but the most common involves several young trees being gathered closely together and tied tightly at the base for several years so they naturally graft together. You must make sure the trees do not become strangulated. If this looks likely, then the tie should be released and another applied.

YOU WILL NEED
rake
scissors
raffia
pot
mesh
wire
wire cutters
soil
scoop
chopstick
branch cutters

Fagus sylvatica purpurea

soil

scoop

rake

chopstick

pot

mesh

wire

wire cutters

scissors

branch cutters

raffia

1 Here five trees that differ slightly in trunk diameter have been selected for the clump. Use scissors to trim off any long roots, leaving a pad of fibrous roots on each tree.

2 Tie the five trees together tightly with raffia. Make the tie very low down on the trunks. They will eventually graft together to form one trunk base.

3 Spread out the trees and position them in the pot.

4 Trim the tops of the trees so that the outer ones are shorter than those in the centre.

BONSAI TIP

A clump of trees looks best in an oval, shallow pot. Here the pot is matt brown, but a glazed pot would also be suitable.

Flowering Tree

Flowering bonsai are very popular, but not every flowering plant is suitable.

It is important to know that when applying the normal techniques of bonsai training the foliage usually tends to decrease in size. However, when growing flowering bonsai bear in mind that flowers and fruit do not reduce in size in the same way. It is therefore essential to select trees that naturally have small flowers and fruit, and which will be in proportion to the size of bonsai that you are growing. Care should be taken to ensure that the growth that will bear flowers is not pruned off before it blooms.

YOU WILL NEED
scissors
knob cutters
wound sealer
rake
pot
mesh
wire
wire cutters
soil
scoop
chopstick

1 You should remove inward-growing branches with scissors.

2 Using knob cutters, prune the very long top growth.

Hamamelis x intermedia

soil

pot

wound sealer

mesh

scoop
rake

wire
cutters

wire

chopstick

scissors

knob
cutters

3 Scrape away the soil with a rake to see where the roots begin to flare out. This will ensure the best blend of trunk to soil surface.

4 Place the tree in a prepared pot and secure in place with wire.

BONSAI TIP
This tree is potted in a cream, glazed pot, which blends with and does not detract from the flowers.

Twin Trunk

Tree seeds often germinate within 60 – 90 cm (2 – 3 ft) of each other: as they grow the distance between them becomes smaller, until eventually they appear as a single tree with two trunks.

In bonsai this can be achieved either by planting two trees very close together or by starting with a tree that already has two trunks. If you plan to begin with two separate trees, they should be tied together tightly with raffia at the base of the trunks for several years. It is best to have two plants of the same species which have differing trunk sizes; one should have a taller and fatter trunk than the other. If a natural pair is available, it must have trunks of different sizes. The smaller trunk should be arranged so that it is alongside the main trunk but slightly behind it. It is important that the two trunk bases are adjacent to each other. The pot for a twin trunk can be any shape, round, oval or rectangular, but not too deep. The tree is planted in a mica pot in such a way that the minor trunk is nearer to the side of the pot than the main trunk.

YOU WILL NEED
branch cutters
wire
wire cutters
scissors
rake
pot
mesh
soil
scoop

Cryptomeria japonica

soil

rake   scoop   wire

pot

wire cutters

mesh   branch cutters   scissors

1 Take off the front branches using branch cutters

2 Remove any small lower branches on the main trunk.

3 Remove any inner branches between the two trunks.

4 Wire the branches on the main trunk and arrange in position.

5 Wire the minor trunk, reposition and prune the top with scissors.

6 Wire the branches on the minor trunk and then position all the branches to give a natural appearance.

Broom

The broom style has an appearance similar to the traditional broom used for sweeping, made from a bunch of twigs tied to a wooden handle. As full-size trees, this style can be seen in parks and gardens all over the world. Initially it was derived from the natural shape of several varieties of Zelkova trees. It is therefore best suited to these trees, but other species can be successfully grown in this style.

The form is based around a straight section of trunk with the branches coming from the top. There may be a continuation of the initial part of the trunk, but it will taper fairly abruptly and have smaller branches emerging along its length.

YOU WILL NEED
branch cutters
scissors
rake
pot
mesh
wire
wire cutters
soil
scoop

Acer palmatum

soil

pot

wire

rake

wire cutters

scoop

mesh

branch cutters

scissors

1 Turn the tree to find the best side to be the front; that is, the side with the most interesting trunk line.

2 Using branch cutters, remove the two small, insignificant low branches.

3 Take out any branches that cross over another branch or the trunk.

4 Prune any heavy side branches.

BONSAI TIP

Plant into a glazed oval or rectangular pot. The hard pruning will encourage the tree to sprout shoots from all areas. Given two or three years of careful trimming and pinching shoots, a well-balanced tree should result.

5 Trim out excess side branches.

6 Cut out the end tips on the apex.

Forest or Group

A group or forest is normally made up of at least five trees. The number should always be odd because this tends to give a more balanced appearance. The forest is probably the hardest style to arrange in a natural-looking way. Your arrangement must re-create the feeling of being in the forest, even though you will be viewing it from the outside.

BONSAI TIP
Prepare the pot in advance, making sure that it is clean, the drainage holes are covered with mesh and include plenty of wires for securing the trees to the pot. The long, shallow, matt-brown pot sets off the group of trees well. Trees in a group look better if they are planted close together.

YOU WILL NEED
pot
mesh
wire
wire cutters
soil
scoop
branch cutters
rake
scissors

Larix leptolepis

pot

wire   *mesh*

scissors   *branch cutters*   *rake*   *wire cutters*   *scoop*

soil

You can use a variety of trees to make a group, but you will find it easier to create a pleasing arrangement if you stick with the same species. In the wild, however, groups are often made up of mixed species, so give it a try: it can be very successful. It is important that the group is realistic and gives the impression of depth and perspective. When viewed from any direction no three trees should be in a straight line and none of the trunks should be completely hidden behind another. Suitable pots would be shallow ovals or rectangles, but you can use a thin slab of slate or rock if you wish.

1 Choose a dominant tree as the main tree in the group and remove its lower branches with concave branch cutters.

2 Having prepared the pot, position the main tree just right of centre.

3 Place the second-largest tree close to the main tree and on its right. You may have to trim some branches so that they sit close together, but not so close as to become confused with each other.

4 Having trimmed both branches and roots to suit, place the third tree close to the second, again on the right. The trees should not be in a straight line when viewed from the side.

Complete with the remaining trees on the left, with the smaller trees to the outside of the group.

Trim back all remaining long shoots to give a tidy, balanced appearance.

Jin

In bonsai, the word *jin* refers to a dead branch that has lost its bark. In the wild, dead branches would be exposed to the natural elements such as rain and wind, and eventually be bleached by the sun to give a natural silvery-white effect. This effect occurs naturally on many varieties of conifer, especially junipers and pines. Although *jin* does not appear on many deciduous trees, it can often be seen on oaks.

YOU WILL NEED
branch cutters
knife
pliers

Larix leptolepis

pliers

branch
cutters

knife

BONSAI TIP
The finished *jin* should be allowed to dry out naturally and a preservative such as lime/sulphur applied.

The reason for creating *jin* by artificial means on bonsai is to create a feeling of substantial age. If carried out correctly, the effect can be dramatic. When pruning a branch on a conifer, always leave a stump several inches long so that it can be converted into a *jin*. The best time to create *jin* is during the summer when the sap movement is at its greatest, because this makes the removal of the bark easier. When you have made the *jin*, you should leave it to dry in the sun before applying a coat of lime/sulphur, which will bleach and preserve the wood. This should be reapplied once or twice a year during the summer to maintain the weather resistance of the *jin*. The *jin* can then be refined by carving and smoothing with fine sandpaper until a truly natural effect is achieved. Remember that the *jin* must always be in proportion to the other branches with foliage.

1 The two branches on the left are the ones chosen to be jinned.

2 Using branch cutters, cut them both off leaving two long stumps.

3 Cut around the bark at the base of each stump with a knife.

4 Use the knife to slit the bark to the end of each stump.

5 Lift the bark with the tip of the knife and peel it off.

6 The ends can now be broken back with pliers to give a natural, weathered look to the stumps.

Wrap-around

A wrap-around is simply a technique used to achieve an aged appearance in a short time. It is the art of attaching a young plant to an old piece of driftwood.

The piece of driftwood should be solid and have any soft or rotten areas cut away. It must then be soaked in clear wood preservative for several months so that every part of the wood is treated. The preservative must be safe for plants. The young live plant is then tied closely to the dead wood with raffia or string and the branches positioned to create a tree form.

YOU WILL NEED
driftwood
wire
wire cutters
pliers
raffia
pot
mesh
rake
soil
chopstick
branch cutters
scissors

driftwood

soil

mesh

chopstick

raffia

rake

scissors

pliers

branch cutters

wire

pot

wire cutters

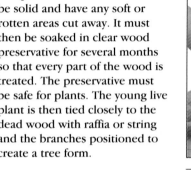

1 The chosen tree here is *Juniperus chinensis*. Prepare the wood as detailed in the introduction.

2 Using pliers, tie the base of the plant to the rear of the piece of wood with wire, and twist tight.

3 Tie the rest of the trunk to the wood with raffia. Space the ties so that the trunk of the juniper is securely fixed to the wood.

4 Wire the tree into the pot.

5 Apply wire to the juniper branches.

6 Position the branches so that they all follow the same pattern.

BONSAI TIP
The finished tree needs time to mature, and the wood needs to be refined over a period of one or two years. The wood also needs to be treated with lime/sulphur to preserve and whiten it. The raffia will eventually be removed when the tree has bonded with the wood.

Shari

Shari can be thought of as a technique that complements *jin*. It will give a tree an even greater appearance of age when used in conjunction with *jin*. A *shari* is where a tree may have been struck by lightning and the bark on part of the trunk has been stripped off. This is commonly seen on pines and junipers, and often connects one *jin* with another, making an even more dramatic effect.

In bonsai, *shari* are created by stripping the bark from part of the trunk. This should be carried out with care as the tree depends on its bark to survive. Always leave enough bark to enable the tree to support the branches that remain, and treat the stripped areas with lime/sulphur to preserve and bleach the heartwood. The best time to make *shari* is during the summer when the sap flow is at its greatest, allowing the bark to be stripped easily.

YOU WILL NEED
felt-tipped pen
knife
pliers
brush

1 This *jin* and the other wounds, which are from a previous pruning, can be refined and made to look more natural.

pliers

knife

Pinus mugo

BONSAI TIP
The *shari* should be treated with lime/sulphur solution, which will preserve and bleach the wood. Given time, a *shari* can be refined by carving and sanding until a mature and striking effect is created.

2 The bark is going to be stripped off down the side and front of the trunk to simulate the appearance of being struck by lightning. Mark the area to be removed with a felt-tipped pen.

3 Cut into the bark with a sharp knife along the marked line. Put just enough pressure on the knife so that you do not go any deeper than the heartwood.

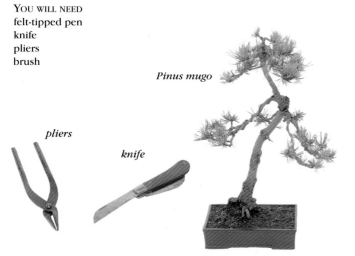

4 Using the tip of the knife, peel back the bark and strip it from the marked area of the trunk.

5 Tidy up the base of the *shari* and make sure the stripped area does not extend right down to the soil level, as this will encourage rotting at the base of the trunk.

6 Brush the *shari* clean and smooth with fine sandpaper if required.

Suitable Varieties

In some ways it would be true to say that there is no such thing as indoor bonsai, because the type of material that is used has its origins as a plant that grows outside in the natural environment. The varieties of plants used for bonsai, therefore, are technically outdoor plants.

Whether these subsequently become known as indoor or outdoor plants, depends on the area of the world in which they are going to be grown. If, for example, you wish to grow a tropical species as a bonsai in a temperate climate, you will need to keep it indoors for at least part of the year. Similarly, trees from temperate regions may need to be kept indoors if cultivated in a tropical or sub-tropical area. This book generally deals with trees that are hardy when kept outdoors in a temperate climate. In any event, bonsai should not be subjected to deep freezing – below -4°c (25°F) – which is why in cold winter regions they need the protection of a cold greenhouse or frame. When trees are referred to as indoor trees in this book, it means that they must be kept in a more controlled environment, such as in a house or greenhouse. These, so-called indoor trees, usually need extra warmth and humidity to maintain a healthy growth pattern. They may also be kept outside during the summer when, and if, the climate comes close to the original conditions in which the plant would be grown. Suitable

material for indoor bonsai can be bought at almost any garden centre or supermarket. Tropical or sub-tropical plants that are used as house-plants can often be turned into bonsai. These plants are normally those that have a wealth of green leaves as their dominant feature, but you should always check the trunk to consider whether it would look good when transformed into a tree-like form. You will have to use your imagination to decide if your choice will be suitable as a bonsai. Species used for indoor bonsai vary considerably, and some of the most popular are the many varieties of *Ficus* or fig, the most common of these being *Ficus benjamina* and *Ficus retusa*. Other species frequently used are *Crassula arborescens*, *Nandina domestica*, *Serissa foetida*, *Punica granatum*, as well as *Sageretia theezans*, *Aralia elegantissima*, *Myrtus communis*, fuchsias, gardenias and many more. Trees grown indoors may need more frequent checking of the climatic conditions. Make sure the soil is always kept moist. Spray the foliage regularly to maintain a fairly high humidity to help to keep the leaves healthy.

Ficus wiandii

Aralia elegantissima

Sageretia theezans

BONSAI TIP
Good light is essential for indoor bonsai. This can be provided by using grow lights to supplement the available natural light.

Crassula arborescens

Myrtus communis

Ficus wiandii

The *Ficus wiandii* has a compact growth habit with well-proportioned leaves. Plants may have one or more trunks and generally have an interesting root system. Regular misting of the foliage with water is beneficial and the soil should be kept just moist at all times. Feed lightly, but regularly, during the main growing season from spring to autumn. As shoots grow prune them back to one or two leaves.

YOU WILL NEED
branch cutters
wound sealer
wire
wire cutters
rake
pot
mesh
soil
scoop
chopstick
scissors

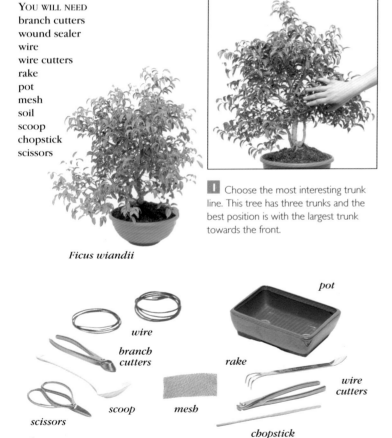

Ficus wiandii

wire

branch cutters

pot

rake

scoop   *mesh*   *wire cutters*

scissors   *chopstick*

1 Choose the most interesting trunk line. This tree has three trunks and the best position is with the largest trunk towards the front.

2 Using branch cutters remove the crossover branch.

3 Cut off any inner branches that do not follow the line. Any white fluid from the wounds will dry up and the wounds should be covered with wound sealer.

4 Remove any heavy upward-growing branches from the tree.

5 Wire the remaining branches.

6 Bend the branches into place, making sure that the branch angles are complementary.

BONSAI TIP
The finished tree is potted in a blue-glazed rectangular pot. As with all the other styling projects, this tree is shown in the early stages of training. It will develop over the next two to three years.

Aralia elegantissima

These plants, commonly known as finger aralia, can have one or more trunks and make a very attractive landscape.

When grown in a group, always make sure that the tallest plant is somewhere in the central third of the arrangement, and that the rest of the plants get progressively smaller towards the sides and rear.

YOU WILL NEED
scissors
pot
mesh
wire
wire cutters
soil
scoop
rake
rocks

Aralia elegantissima

rocks

soil

mesh

scoop

scissors

pot

wire

rake

wire cutters

1 Cut off the lower and inner leaves of the plants using scissors.

2 Place in the prepared pot, arranging the seven trunks so that they are slightly spread out at the top.

3 Add extra soil until the trees are firmly potted.

4 Carefully position several pieces of rock or tufa to give the effect of a miniature landscape.

BONSAI TIP
It is important to mist regularly as the leaves can dry out quickly.

Sageretia theezans

Sageretia theezans is a popular species for indoor bonsai and specimens are normally sold as fully trained trees. This one has grown on and lost its original shape.

These trees have delicate leaves which may lose their moisture and dry out. Regular misting of the foliage should control this situation. The bark comes away in flakes leaving an attractive orange colour. Regular feeding, using half the recommended strength of fertilizers suitable for green-leaf plants, will be beneficial. The roots develop quickly, so repot every year.

YOU WILL NEED
rake
branch cutters
pot
mesh
wire
wire cutters
soil
scoop
scissors

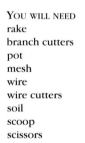
Sageretia theezans

soil
wire
mesh
scissors *branch cutters* *rake* *wire cutters* *scoop* *pot*

1 Having removed the plant from the pot, use branch cutters to cut out the central branch which would otherwise spoil the line of the finished tree.

2 Settle the tree into the pot just off centre and fill up with soil using a scoop.

3 Using scissors, cut back the long shoots, leaving just one or two leaves.

4 Mist the soil and plant to create a high humidity. This species has thin leaves that can dry out quickly after repotting, so do this regularly.

Crassula arborescens

Commonly known as the money tree or jade plant, this plant is often underestimated as bonsai material. Many species of *Crassula* are available and *arborescens* is one of the best.

Crassula arborescens has thick leaves and is strictly a succulent. The leaves and stems hold a large quantity of water, which allows the plant to go for several weeks without showing any signs of wilting. This characteristic makes the plant easy to look after as it needs watering less often than most plants. Even if the plant dries out, wilts and generally looks dehydrated, it will almost always recover once watering has been resumed. Propagation is easy; just break off a leaf, leave until the end is dry (about four days), and lay it on the surface of some dry soil. In about one month the leaf will have sprouted new roots. Do not water until you can see signs of new growth. Feed as with other house-plants, but only with a weak mixture of fertilizer. When controlling the growth of your bonsai *Crassula*, wait until two or three pairs of leaves have been produced and then trim back to one pair. Each time you do this, the growth pattern will double up. That is, each pruned shoot will produce two new shoots. Never allow the *Crassula* to be exposed to frost, because its high water content will freeze and on thawing the tree will just collapse.

You will need
branch cutters
scissors
rake
pot
mesh
soil
scoop
chopstick

Crassula arborescens

soil

pot

mesh

branch cutters

scoop

scissors

rake

chopstick

1 Cut off the left-hand trunk, using branch cutters, so that the main trunk in the centre is dominant.

2 Clean up the remaining stump.

3 Pull off the lower leaves to expose the line of the tree's main trunk.

4 Having removed the leaves, it is clear that the other low branch should be removed. This allows you to see the main trunk at its best.

BONSAI TIP

The appearance of the soil surface can be improved by adding some moss, which is then watered in.

5 Using scissors, reduce the length of the leading shoots.

6 Position in a suitable pot and top up with soil, working it in and around the roots with a chopstick.

Myrtus communis

Commonly known as dwarf myrtle, only young plants of this variety are usually available, but it is relatively easy to train as bonsai. If you can buy some small plants, a miniature landscape can be constructed, using a combination of pot, plants, soil and rocks.

Try to thin out the top growth to achieve a branched structure. It is only too easy to be tempted to "clip" the foliage, but that would be topiary rather than bonsai. You will need to be persistent with the thinning out process, because a dense foliage mass can quickly regrow. This species requires regular misting with water to maintain the health of the foliage, particularly in the summer months. As with most indoor bonsai, this variety can be placed outside in a shady spot in warmer weather. Water when the soil begins to show signs of drying, and never allow the roots to stand in water as they will quickly rot. Good light is important, but never place your tree in direct sunlight shining through a window as this will scorch the leaves.

You will need
rake
scissors
pot
mesh
wire
wire cutters
soil
scoop
rocks

Myrtus communis

soil

pot

rocks

mesh

scissors

rake

scoop

wire

wire cutters

1 Having removed the plants from their pots, rake away the soil to obtain a suitable rootball and expose the trunk base. Using scissors, trim off some of the lower branches so that the trunk lines can be seen.

2 Trim each plant into a tree-like form.

3 Prepare the pot in the normal way and add a layer of soil.

4 Arrange some rocks, in this case tufa, so that there is enough space to plant trees around them and add extra soil.

5 Place the medium-size tree on the left and settle it into the soil.

6 Having placed the smallest tree on the right, plant the largest beside it and to the right of the rock. Make sure that this tree is slightly higher than the others. Never finish up with the tops of all of the trees on the same level. The final effect should be that of a miniature landscape.

Refining Techniques – Broad-leaf Trees

As bonsai mature, similar techniques to those already discussed in this book are employed to refine their shape. However, they will always need some form of pruning.

Minor adjustments can be made to the shape of a tree using the wiring techniques. Young shoots sprout from various places on trunks and branches, and some of these will need to be removed to maintain the mature look of the tree. Tidying up old pruning cuts, removing dead branches and thinning out the branch structure are all essential to ensure continued improvement of your bonsai.

YOU WILL NEED
branch cutters
scissors
wire
wire cutters
wound sealer

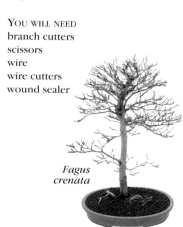

Fagus crenata

scissors

wire cutters

branch cutters

wire

1 Using concave branch cutters, remove stubs left from previous pruning.

2 Cut out small adventitious shoots with scissors.

3 Apply wire to branches that cover the front of the tree.

4 Reposition the branches, one to the right and the other to the left, and seal all cuts with wound sealer.

Refining Techniques – Conifers

As with deciduous trees, refining techniques include pruning shoots, cutting out unwanted branches and thinning foliage. It also includes the introduction of *jin*, *shari* and other artificial ageing processes.

The relationship of one branch to another and the space between them is important, because this enables the tree to be seen at its best. Creating spaces between branches also allows the sunlight to reach all the foliage and this will lead to healthier, more compact growth. Pinch out young growth with your fingers but use scissors for hardened growth.

YOU WILL NEED
scissors
branch cutters
wire
wire cutters

Juniperus chinensis

branch cutters

wire cutters

scissors

wire

1 Use scissors to remove all downward growth.

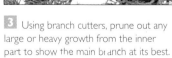

2 Similarly, remove all upward growth.

3 Using branch cutters, prune out any large or heavy growth from the inner part to show the main branch at its best.

4 Gather up the foliage in bunches and pinch the tips off using fingers or tweezers to thin out the leaves.

Watering

If your trees are kept outside where rain can water them, you need to worry only when it does not rain. Use a watering-can with a fine rose or if you have a large collection of trees use a hose, which should also have a fine rose attached.

The frequency of watering will depend on many things. A strong wind or sun, or a combination of both, can quickly dry out the soil, so you must monitor moisture levels in the soil regularly. Indoor trees require slightly different watering techniques. It is easy to water by just "dunking" the whole pot into a bowl, completely covering the soil with water. Wait until the bubbles stop rising, remove from the water and allow to drain. Indoor trees can also be watered using a small watering-can. Indoor trees often also require extra humidity around the foliage. To achieve this spray the leaves regularly or place the pot on a shallow dish or tray containing a layer of absorbent granules, which are kept wet, so that as the water evaporates it drifts up and around the foliage. This slows down transpiration of water from the leaves and therefore decreases the chance of the leaves shrivelling.

YOU WILL NEED
bowl
watering-can
sprayer

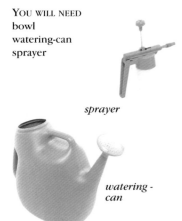

sprayer

watering - can

2 Use a watering-can with a fine rose to water the soil and roots.

1 Fill a bowl with water and immerse the pot in the water until the bubbles cease to rise; remove from the water and leave to drain.

3 The same watering-can may be used to water the foliage on a weekly basis, particularly if there has not been any rain for a while.

4 You can also water with a pressure sprayer or with a hose fitted with a fine rose.

Feeding

Regular feeding at the correct time of year, with the correct fertilizer, is essential to maintain good healthy growth. A certain amount of fertilizer is washed out by watering so a regular input of nutrients is required.

YOU WILL NEED
fertilizer – granules, pellets, liquid
tweezers
watering-can
sprayer

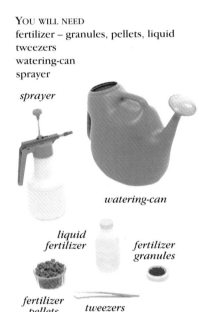

sprayer

watering-can

liquid fertilizer

fertilizer granules

fertilizer pellets

tweezers

Fertilizers come in a variety of forms, as soluble powders, slow-release granules, pellets and liquids, and these can be applied by spraying onto the foliage, watering into the soil or by placing pellets on the soil surface. Pellets are a slow-release fertilizer and will take care of feeding requirements for several weeks at a time. Soluble powder and liquid feeds are applied to the soil with a watering-can. Foliar feeding can be carried out using a liquid foliar feed and applying with an atomizing sprayer. Never apply more fertilizer than the recommended dose. General feeding should take place from early spring to late summer, but an autumn feed with a very low – or no – nitrogen content will harden off the current year's growth and help the tree through the winter. Most fertilizers contain nitrogen (N), phosphorus (P) and potassium (K), which are always indicated on the package as an NPK ratio, for example, NPK 6:12:10. Nitrogen is essential for leaf and stem growth, and is responsible for the rich green colours of the leaves. Too much nitrogen will make the tree produce too much long growth, which is not required for bonsai. Use a balanced fertilizer with a fairly low N content. Phosphorus is mostly responsible for healthy root growth, but it also helps the growth of buds and in the protection against diseases and adverse winter conditions. Potassium (potash) encourages the formation of flowers and fruit, and is a vital component in the fight against disease. It also helps with hardening off growth before the winter. Most commercial fertilizers contain all three main nutrients plus some trace elements, which provide the trees with all the other minor, though essential, nutrients. There is one type of fertilizer that is normally only obtainable from bonsai nurseries and which has an NPK ratio of 0:10:10. This is an autumn feed, which will harden off the current season's growth in readiness for the winter.

2 Make sure the fertilizer has been absorbed into the water, then apply the mixture to the soil.

3 Pellets made of rapeseed cake can be applied by laying them on the soil surface with tweezers or fingers.

4 After placing the pellets, water over them to start the feeding process.

1 You can apply liquid fertilizers to the roots using a watering-can. Tip the fertilizer into the can.

Insect Pests

Bonsai are susceptible to the same insect pests as full-size trees. To help prevent infestation, the application of a systemic insecticide twice a year is beneficial. Systemic products are absorbed into the plant and give it protection for several months. A winter wash can be applied to deciduous trees to eliminate any overwintering eggs and grubs.

Vine weevil

The vine weevil grub can kill a tree quickly because it feeds on and destroys the roots. Treat with a soil insecticide at the first signs and if possible repot, making sure that all of the grubs are removed. The adult vine weevil hides away in rubbish, beneath pots and staging during the day, and emerges at night to eat large holes in the edge of leaves. Treat with an appropriate insecticide.

Adult vine weevil (Otiorhynchus sulcatus)

Vine weevil grub

Scale insect

Scale insects can be inconspicuous until they begin to produce eggs. When this happens, the limpet-like shells lift and a white, fluffy, sticky mass appears from beneath. Combat them with systemic insecticide and pick off the large adult insects. A cotton bud (swab) soaked in methylated spirit (denatured alcohol) can be very effective for rubbing scale from the trunks of bonsai.

Scale insect (Hemiptera: Coccoidea)

Aphids

Aphids come in many forms, but greenfly, blackfly and whitefly are the most common. They can be treated with a systemic insecticide. The most troublesome pest for indoor bonsai may be whitefly, but regular applications of some form of insecticide will control the pest.

Greenfly, blackfly and whitefly (aphids)

Woolly aphid

Woolly aphid is a particular problem on beech and pine. It looks like a white, fluffy, sticky mass, and can be removed by spraying regularly with an insecticide.

Woolly aphid (Eriosoma lanigerum)

Red spider mite

Red spider mite is a tiny red insect which is not normally detected until very fine webs appear at the junctions of the trunk and branches. They often attack junipers, but can also cause a problem on many other trees, including indoor varieties. Treatment is in the form of an insecticide, which again can be applied on a regular basis.

Red spider mite (Acarina: Tetranychidae)

All pests can be kept under control by hygienic practices, which will avoid the excessive use of insecticides. Insecticides should be used only if other removal methods fail to work.

Diseases

Most diseases found in bonsai are the same as those which affect full-size trees and are mostly of the fungus family. Fungal infections can be reduced if hygienic practices are adhered to when preparing trees, pots and soil, and also with general cleanliness.

Routine spraying with systemic fungicides will control most of the common fungal infections. You may also spray with copper fungicide, alternating with the systemic variety, as an extra precaution.

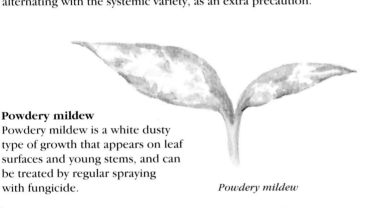

Powdery mildew
Powdery mildew is a white dusty type of growth that appears on leaf surfaces and young stems, and can be treated by regular spraying with fungicide.

Powdery mildew

Damping off
Damping off is where seedlings begin to rot at the base of the stem, resulting in the seedling falling over and dying. Spray with copper-based fungicide.

Damping off

Rust
Rust appears on leaves as slightly raised orange/yellow spots and any affected leaves should be removed and destroyed. You should also spray with a zinc-based fungicide.

Rust

Verticillium wilt
Verticillium wilt is a disease that causes die-back in maples. It attacks the sapwood and is difficult to detect, and most trees should be treated with a systemic fungicide as a preventive measure.

Verticillium wilt

Peach leaf curl
Peach leaf curl can be a problem on trees of the *Prunus* family and appears as reddish-brown blistery shapes on the leaves. These quickly multiply, causing the leaves to curl up into distorted shapes. Treat with a copper-based fungicide.

Peach leaf curl

Grey mould
Grey mould is a fungus that occurs on leaves of plants which are kept in conditions of high humidity. It is possible to control by increasing ventilation and spraying with a systemic fungicide. Always make sure that the directions on the packaging are adhered to closely, and if there are any safety precautions, follow them to the letter.

Grey mould

Preparing for Exhibition – Trunks and Branches

If you are planning to exhibit your bonsai, you should carry out a few tasks to tidy up and improve their appearance. Your trees will, hopefully, always look good, but when showing them off they must be at their very best.

Clean the trunk and branches by brushing, washing or both, and remove any damaged leaves or die-back. Loose, flaky bark should be removed, and any signs of disease or insect attack also removed or treated. Some junipers can be enhanced by lightly rubbing vegetable oil on to the bark to bring out the colour.

YOU WILL NEED
tweezers
toothbrush
sprayer

Juniperus chinensis

tweezers

toothbrush

sprayer

1 Remove odd bits of dead bark from the trunk with tweezers.

2 Brush clean with a dry, stiff brush.

3 Using the brush and water, clean the tree of algae.

4 Spraying with water while brushing will wash away any loose debris.

90

Soil Surface and Pots

The appearance of the soil surface and the cleanliness of the pots is of utmost importance when preparing bonsai for exhibition.

Dead leaves should be removed from the surface of the soil, along with any other unsightly bits and pieces. Brush the soil surface clean and add some moss, so that a natural effect is obtained. Pots should be brushed or washed clean and allowed to dry. To enhance the appearance and colour of the pot, apply a film of vegetable oil with a lint-free cloth.

YOU WILL NEED
soil
moss
vegetable oil
lint-free cloth
brush

Juniperus rigida

moss

soil

vegetable oil

brush

1 Brush the soil surface and top up with soil if necessary.

2 Add some moss and press it into the soil surface while spraying. This helps the moss to establish quickly and results in a very natural look.

3 Brush the sides and rim of the pot to remove loose dust and then wash off any remaining dirt.

4 Using a lint-free cloth soaked with vegetable oil, wipe the pot to bring out the texture and colour.

Displaying Bonsai

Take great care when displaying your bonsai inside the home, to see that everything involved in that display complements and enhances the appearance of the tree.

Good-quality display tables are available commercially and can be bought in a variety of shapes and sizes. But if you feel that you have the skill and ability, you may be able to make a stand yourself. Bamboo matting, gravel and many other materials may be used in the display of bonsai, and it is left to the individual to design a suitable setting. However, if you need some inspiration there are many books on Japanese design and culture.

This type of rosewood stand is suitable for the more upright styles of bonsai.

An antique stand is ideal for displaying cascading bonsai.

The same stand with a cascade-style Juniperus procumbens.

Rosewood stand with Juniperus squamata *"Meyeri".*

Outdoor Bonsai Display

Display systems for bonsai kept outside can be more rustic in appearance. Timber benches treated with preservative are ideal, and can be supported either on timber legs or concrete blocks. The latter will remove the possibility of rot setting in or the benches collapsing.

The need for strong display benching is important, and you should also see that the size and weight of benching is kept in proportion to the trees displayed. The best height for displaying bonsai is roughly eye level so that the trees can be seen at their best. This may not always be possible if you have a large collection, and it would be a good idea to vary the height of each stand to suit each tree. The main aim should be to give a pleasing overall effect while providing you with ease of access for maintenance.

Below left: Five trees displayed in a small space on two different types of timber stands.
Bottom left: A single pole stand which is 1 m (3 ft) high.

Below right: Multiple bonsai in one unit, creating an interesting display.
Bottom right: The author's bonsai display in Sussex, England.

Winter Preparation

Whether or not your bonsai need protection for the winter depends on the climate where you live. If your trees are going to be exposed to conditions below freezing, then you may have to take extra precautions. These may include placing trees in a greenhouse, shade tunnel or just under the benching.

When placing under benches the trees should always be put on some form of timber staging to keep them off the ground, and for extra protection cover the front, sides and back of the benching. Small trees can be placed in containers filled to the brim with peat so that the rootball and pot are covered. These methods for extra winter protection should only be carried out if it becomes necessary, because over-protection of normally hardy species can lead to problems with new growth in the spring.

YOU WILL NEED
greenhouse shading
plastic basket
display stand and timber slats
humus matter

BONSAI TIP
Check moisture levels in pots during the winter. Protect them from heavy rain and keep the soil just damp at all times.

1 Two trees are placed on timber slats beneath the normal bonsai display bench.

2 Cover the front and sides (and rear if it is open) with greenhouse shade netting. Here it is partially covered to show the placement of the trees, but it will be completely covered when the temperature falls below freezing.

3 You can protect roots by placing the pots in a box or basket filled with humus.

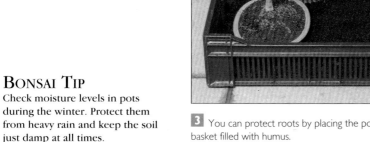

4 Here the two trees have their pots and roots protected from severe winter frosts.

Hygiene

Cleanliness is extremely important when preparing hardy trees for the dormant season. Clear away all dead leaves because these make good hiding-places for insects and breeding places for diseases.

This includes leaves and rubbish on the soil surrounding your trees as well as the debris that collects on the display benches. All of these actions will lead to a healthier collection of bonsai.

YOU WILL NEED
stiff brush
vegetable oil
soft brush
tweezers

BONSAI TIP
Check on cleanliness throughout the year – it will help to maintain healthy trees.

1 Leaves and rubbish on and around your trees can harbour all sorts of unwanted insects and diseases.

2 The removal of rubbish not only makes the trees look better, it keeps them healthier too.

3 Here you can see that the pot is dirty and there is fallen foliage on the soil surface.

4 The removal of debris, and cleaning and oiling of the pot, will help to keep the tree healthier as well as improving its appearance.

INDEX